EXPLORING CHICAGO

EXPLORING
CHICAGO

A LOCAL'S GUIDE TO THE BEST ATTRACTIONS, NEIGHBORHOODS, FOOD AND HIDDEN GEMS.

KRISTEN PETTRY

CONTENTS

INTRODUCTION

Welcome to Chicago, the Windy City, my home-town. This vibrant metropolis, located on the shores of Lake Michigan, boasts a rich tapestry of cultural influences, making it a melting pot of traditions and communities. From the iconic deep-dish pizza to the soaring skyline views, the city is famous for its deep-rooted history in jazz and blues music and its significant contributions to art, architecture, and culinary innovation.

The skyline, dominated by iconic structures like the Willis Tower, showcases a blend of modern and historic design. The city's neighborhoods each offer unique flavors, from the artsy streets of Wicker Park to the historic charm of Hyde Park. Chicago's culinary scene is equally dynamic, and it has a thriving restaurant culture that celebrates a range of international cuisines. Additionally, the city hosts various festivals, musical performances, and art shows, showcasing its creative spirit and commitment to community involvement.

This book is not intended to give you every detail about Chicago, but it will undoubtedly help you make the most of your visit to the Windy City. We will journey through the heart of Chicago, touring

some of its historic neighborhoods, celebrated land-marks, and explore the cultural nuances that make it a truly remarkable city. You will learn about the must-see attractions, savor the local cuisine, and easily navigate the public transportation system. With practical tips and insightful recommendations, this guide aims to help you immerse yourself in the essence of Chicago, creating unforgettable memories along the way.

Chicago is a city that truly comes alive with activities and experiences for everyone. Whether you're strolling through the iconic Millennium Park, taking a scenic boat ride on Lake Michigan, or delving into the colorful art scene in Pilsen, there's no shortage of adventure. The city's vibrant atmosphere and friendly locals make it an inviting destination for exploration and enjoyment. Now, let's start exploring Chicago!

The Chicago River

A BRIEF HISTORY OF CHICAGO

Chicago, nestled on the southwestern shore of Lake Michigan, has a rich history that spans centuries. The area was initially inhabited by various Native American tribes, notably the Potawatomi, who thrived on the land's resources. European exploration began in the late 17th century, with French explorers like Jacques Marquette and Louis Jolliet being among the first to traverse the region in 1673. Jean Baptiste Point du Sable is recognized as the city's first permanent non-Indigenous settler.

The city's formal inception came in 1833 when it was incorporated as a town with 350 residents. Its location was strategically significant due to its access to waterways and railroads, which fueled rapid growth. By the mid-19th century, Chicago had blossomed into a bustling city, attracting immigrants from Europe seeking opportunities. The Great Fire of 1871 was pivotal in Chicago's history, destroying a large part of the city and paving the way for innovative architectural advancements. The legend of the Great Chicago Fire of 1871 suggests that a cow owned by Mrs. O'Leary kicked over a lantern, igniting the blaze that devastated a large portion of the city. While this story has become a part of Chicago folklore, historians debate its accuracy, noting that

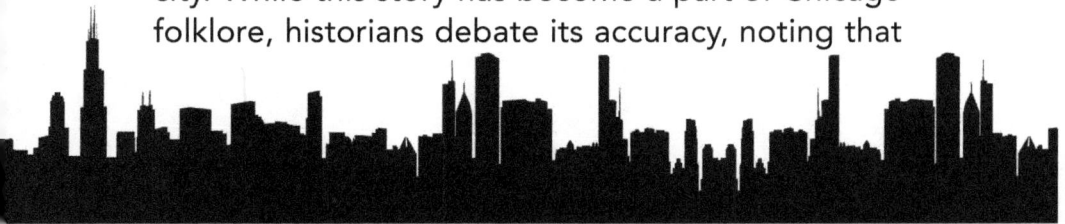

the fire's true cause remains unknown. Regardless of the cow's involvement, the fire resulted in significant loss of life and property, leading to major changes in fire safety regulations and urban planning. The event has since become a pivotal chapter in Chicago's history, symbolizing destruction and the city's remarkable resilience and rebuilding efforts.

In the aftermath of the Great Chicago Fire and into the early 20th century, visionary architect and planner Daniel Burnham helped shape the city's rebirth. His 1909 Plan of Chicago - often called the Burnham Plan - laid the groundwork for modern city planning, with proposals for lakefront parks, grand boulevards, and cohesive zoning. Burnham's famous motto, "Make no little plans," became a rallying cry for ambition and transformation. His vision continues to influence how Chicago balances beauty, function, and civic pride.

Burnham's Plan

As the 20th century approached, Chicago emerged as a cultural and economic hub, known for its vibrant music scene, particularly jazz and blues. Chicago's jazz and blues music has profoundly influenced the genre's evolution and spread across America and beyond. The city's vibrant clubs, such as the legendary Kingston Mines and the historic Cotton Club, became breeding grounds for iconic musicians like Muddy Waters, Howlin' Wolf, and Louis Armstrong. The Great Migration (when African Americans relocated from the South to northern cities), and the unique blend of African American cultural expressions helped establish Chicago as a pivotal hub for these music styles, leading to the development of sub-genres like Chicago blues. Today, the city celebrates its jazz heritage through festivals, events, and dedicated venues, ensuring that the sound of jazz remains an integral part of Chicago's cultural identity.

The city played a crucial role during the Prohibition era, becoming infamous for its organized crime. Al Capone is often associated with the roaring 1920s and the Prohibition era in Chicago. Known for his sharp suits and charismatic personality, Capone rose to power as the leader of the Chicago Outfit, a criminal organization involved in illegal activities such as bootlegging, gambling, and vice. The St. Valentine's Day Massacre, which occurred on February 14, 1929, remains one of the most infamous events in Chicago's gangster history and is often linked to Al Capone's criminal empire. Despite his criminal lifestyle, he was known for his philanthropic efforts, often donating to local charities and hospitals, earning him a mixed reputation among some Chicagoans. Capone's life and exploits continue to fascinate people today, often depicted in films, books, and documentaries about the gangster era. His reign ended in 1931 when he was convicted of tax evasion, but the legacy of organized crime in Chicago continued.

Al Capone

The latter half of the century saw significant social changes in Chicago, particularly through the civil rights movement, which profoundly influenced the city's diverse communities. Activism surged as individuals and groups, including the Chicago chapter of the Southern Christian Leadership Conference (SCLC) and the Black Panthers, organized campaigns to challenge systemic racism and advocate for civil rights. Notable events, such as the Chicago Freedom Movement led by Dr. Martin Luther King Jr., aimed to address issues like housing discrimination and economic inequality. This period also witnessed increased collaboration among various ethnic groups fighting for justice, resulting in a more unified front against oppression. The activism of this era not only reshaped the social fabric of Chicago but also laid the groundwork for ongoing struggles for equity, leaving a lasting legacy on the city's identity. The effects of these changes are still evident today, as Chicago continues to be a mosaic of cultures and identities, reflecting the struggles and triumphs of the past.

The Chicago River itself has a rich and dynamic history that dates back to the city's founding in the early 19th century. Originally, the river was a natural waterway that played a crucial role in the development of Chicago as a trading and transportation hub. The Chicago River actually flows backward due to a monumental engineering project completed in the late 19th century that reversed its flow away from Lake Michigan, helping to improve the city's water quality. Over the years, the river has undergone extensive modifications, including the construction of canals and the installation of locks to accommodate growing maritime traffic. The Chicago River is also home to a variety of wildlife, including fish species like salmon and carp, making it a popular spot for fishing. Furthermore, it features a stunning 1.5-mile-long Riverwalk, which offers scenic views, dining options, and recreational activities, enhancing the urban landscape. Each St. Patrick's Day the Chicago River turns green. This festive event began in 1962 when local plumbers used a dye to locate pollution in the river, and the vibrant green color quickly became a symbol of the holiday. The dye used is environmentally safe and typically takes about 24 hours to fade, ensuring that the river returns to its natural state. On the morning of St. Patrick's Day, crowds gather along the riverbanks to witness the transformation, making it one of the most photographed events in Chicago. This unique celebration not only showcases the city's Irish heritage but also draws tourists from around the world, contributing to Chicago's cultural vibrancy.

Current-day Chicago is a vibrant metropolis known for its diverse culture, rich history, and dynamic economy. It is the third-largest city in the United States, home to over 2.7 million residents who represent a wide array of ethnic backgrounds. Chicago is known for its iconic skyline, rich history, and cultural institutions. Its legacy is reflected in its neighborhoods, each telling a story of the waves of immigrants who have called this city home.

MUSEUMS, TRAILS, AND HIDDEN GEMS

Chicago is home to a diverse array of world-class museums and unforgettable attractions that show-case its rich culture, history, and creativity. From towering dinosaurs and priceless art collections to scenic lakefront trails and lush indoor gardens, the city offers experiences for every interest and every season. In this section, we'll explore some of the must-visit museums, outdoor adventures, and hidden gems that make Chicago a truly dynamic and inspiring destination.

The Art Institute of Chicago

The Art Institute of Chicago was founded in 1879, is not only one of the oldest and largest art museums in the United States but also a cornerstone of Chicago's cultural identity. Its vast collection boasts over 300,000 works of art, making it a treasure trove for art enthusiasts. The museum is renowned for its extensive holdings of Impressionist and Post-Impressionist paintings, including iconic works by artists such as Claude Monet, Vincent van Gogh, and Georges Seurat. Additionally, the collection encompasses

American art, featuring pieces by Edward Hopper and Grant Wood and Old Masters like Rembrandt and Vermeer. The museum's decorative arts section showcases stunning European and American craftsmanship, while its Asian art collection highlights the rich traditions of East Asia. Visitors are greeted by the museum's famous bronze lion statues, which stand guard at the entrance, symbolizing both strength and the city's dedication to the arts. Beyond its impressive collections, the Art Institute is committed to community involvement through various educational programs, exhibitions, and public events designed to enhance public engagement and deepen appreciation for the arts. The museum also houses a renowned research library and provides resources for scholars and art lovers alike, ensuring its role as a vital educational institution in the heart of Chicago.

The Art Institute of Chicago

The Field Museum of Natural History

The Field Museum of Natural History is one of the largest natural history museums in the world, renowned for its extensive collection of over 24 million specimens. Established in 1893, the museum features exhibits on anthropology, paleontology, geology, and botany. Some of the most popular exhibits at the Chicago Field Museum include Sue, the largest and most complete T. rex skeleton, which captivates visitors with its impressive size and history. The Ancient Egypt exhibit showcases mummies and artifacts, allowing guests to explore the mysteries of this fascinating civilization. The Grainger Hall of Gems features a stunning collection of gemstones and minerals, while the Hall of Animal Habitats presents diverse ecosystems and the animals that inhabit them. Visitors can also view the actual taxidermy specimens of the infamous lions, known as "The Ghost" and "The Darkness." These lions gained notoriety for their unusual behavior of hunting humans, leading to a dramatic series of events that ultimately captured the attention of the world. There is even a movie featuring Val Kilmer and Michael Douglas based on true events. All these exhibits and more, highlight the museum's commitment to showcasing natural history and engaging audiences.

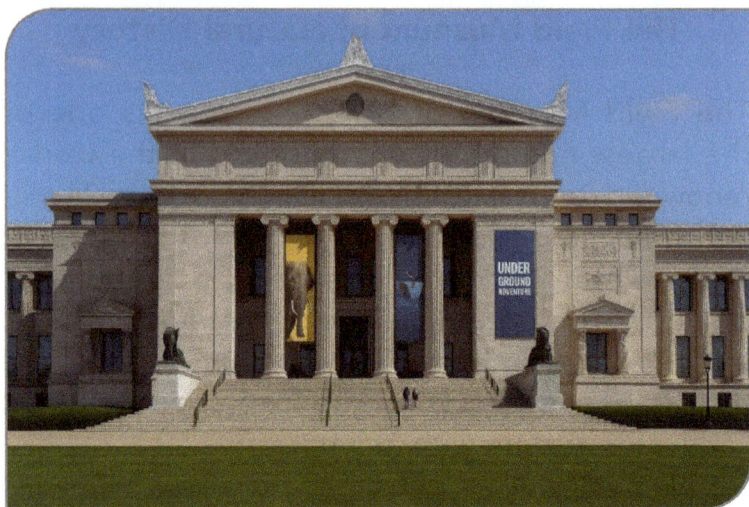

The Field Museum of Natural History

The Chicago Museum of Science and Industry

The Museum of Science and Industry is housed in the historic Palace of Fine Arts from the 1893 World's Columbian Exposition and stands as one of the largest science museums in the world. Spanning over 400,000 square feet, the museum encompasses a vast array of exhibits that delve into various scientific disciplines, including technology, biology, physics, and engineering. Among its most notable attractions is a full-size replica of a coal mine, which allows visitors to experience the history and processes of coal mining firsthand. The museum also features the U-505 submarine, a captured German U-boat from World War II, which offers a unique glimpse into naval warfare and submarine technology. Another highlight is the Great Train Story exhibit, which illustrates the evolution of transportation and its significant impact on society through an elaborate model train display. The Chicago Museum of Science and Industry prioritizes hands-on learning and interactive experiences, making it an ideal destination for families, school groups, and curious minds of all ages. With numerous workshops, demonstrations, and exhibits designed to engage visitors, the museum fosters a sense of wonder and exploration. I highly recommend the U-505 tour, where guests can explore the submarine and learn about its historical context, enhancing their understanding of maritime history. This commitment to education and interactive learning solidifies the museum's reputation as a must-visit attraction in Chicago.

Museum of Science and Industry

The Shedd Aquarium

The Shedd Aquarium, one of the largest indoor aquariums in the world, is a remarkable destination that houses more than 32,000 animals from over 1,500 species. Since its opening in 1930, the aquarium has captivated visitors with various engaging exhibits highlighting the beauty and diversity of aquatic life. Among the most popular attractions is the Caribbean Reef, where guests can observe colorful fish and vibrant coral ecosystems in a stunning underwater environment. The Amazon Rising exhibit brings the rich wildlife of the Amazon River to life, featuring fascinating creatures such as piranhas, anacondas, and exotic birds, showcasing the unique biodiversity of this vital ecosystem. Another highlight is the Wild Reef, which immerses visitors in a thriving coral reef habitat populated with sharks, rays, and numerous other marine species, providing an unforgettable glimpse into the underwater world. For a hands-on experience, the Polar Play Zone allows guests to interact with playful sea otters and charming penguins, enhancing both enjoyment and education.

The Shedd Aquarium is also dedicated to conservation, education, and research, offering immersive experiences such as animal encounters and behind-the-scenes tours that deepen visitors' connections to aquatic life. Additionally, various programs and events aim to foster a sense of responsibility for marine ecosystems, making the aquarium not just a place to observe but also a hub for learning and advocacy for ocean conservation.

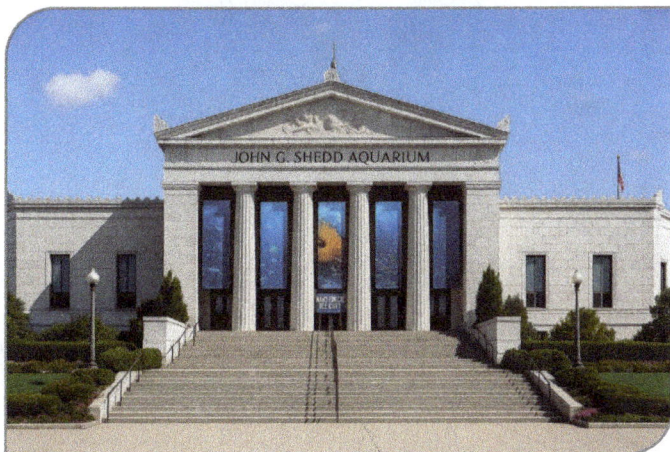

The Shedd Aquarium

The Adler Planetarium

The Adler Planetarium is a premier destination for astronomy enthusiasts and curious minds alike. Just a stone's throw away from the Shedd Aquarium, the Planetarium offers a captivating experience with its engaging exhibits, state-of-the-art theaters, and interactive displays that explore the universe and its wonders. Visitors can enjoy breathtaking shows in the dome theater, learn about celestial phenomena, and participate in hands-on activities that inspire a deeper understanding of space. The planetarium also hosts special events and programs that cater to all ages, making it a vital part of Chicago's cultural landscape.

Adler Planetarium

Iconic Trails and Unexpected Treasures

While exploring the Museum Campus, don't miss the chance to experience the Chicago Lakefront Trail. This scenic 18-mile path runs along the shoreline of Lake Michigan, connecting many of Chicago's most famous parks, beaches, and attractions. Whether you're walking, biking, or simply enjoying the views, the trail offers stunning vistas of the skyline and lakefront, making it one of the city's most beloved outdoor experiences.

For another unforgettable stroll, head to the Chicago Riverwalk. Stretching along the south bank of the Chicago River, this lively waterfront path features restaurants, public art, and spectacular views of the city's iconic architecture. It's a vibrant counterpart to the Lakefront Trail and offers a completely different perspective on the heart of downtown.

If you're ready for a change of pace, venture indoors to the Garfield Park Conservatory. Often called "landscape art under glass," it's one of the largest and most breathtaking botanical conservatories in the United States. Inside, you'll find a series of lush greenhouses filled with exotic plants, tropical gardens, and colorful seasonal flower shows. Best of all, admission is free (with donations appreciated), making it a peaceful, low-cost retreat for plant lovers, architecture buffs, and anyone looking to escape into nature.

Garfield Park Conservatory

EXPLORING ARCHITECTURAL AND HISTORIC LANDMARKS

The city's skyline features many significant architectural structures. Chicago was a pioneer in the development of the modern skyscraper, with innovations like steel-frame construction and the elevator. The city is home to iconic buildings that showcase various architectural styles, from the Gothic Revival of the Tribune Tower to the sleek modernism of the Willis Tower. Chicago's skyline has influenced urban planning and architectural design worldwide, serving as a model for other cities aiming to create cohesive and visually striking skylines.

Daniel Burnham was a pivotal figure in shaping Chicago's architectural landscape in the late 19th and early 20th centuries. As an architect and urban planner, he was instrumental in the development of the Chicago Plan, a visionary initiative that aimed to enhance the city's beauty and functionality. One of Daniel Burnham's most famous quotes is, "Make no little plans; they have no magic to stir men's blood and probably themselves will not be realized." This quote encapsulates his belief in the importance of visionary thinking and ambition in urban planning and architecture. Burnham emphasized the need

for grand ideas that inspire communities and drive progress, reflecting his commitment to creating a magnificent and functional urban environment. His approach to planning and architecture not only shaped Chicago but also influenced cities across America, encouraging planners to think big and strive for excellence in their designs.

The skyline not only defines the city's identity but also attracts millions of visitors each year, eager to explore these iconic structures and their architectural legacy. It would be nearly impossible to cover them all in one visit. In this guide, we will look at some of the top architectural and historic landmarks to explore during your time in Chicago.

Willis Tower

The Willis Tower, formerly known as the Sears Tower, is one of Chicago's most iconic landmarks. It was once the tallest building in the world, standing at 1,450 feet (442 meters). Located in the Loop, and completed in 1973, it features 110 floors and is renowned for its distinctive black glass façade. The tower houses offices, observation decks, and the Skydeck, which offers breathtaking views of the city and beyond, including the thrilling "Ledge," a glass balcony extending four feet outside the building. Willis Tower remains a significant symbol of Chicago's skyline and attracts millions of visitors each year. Chicago humor about the Willis Tower's name change from Sears often pokes fun at how stubborn locals can be. One joke is that the only thing taller than the Willis Tower is the list of people who still insist on calling it Sears. For most of us who live in Chicago, it is pronounced "Sears" but spelled "Willis".

Willis Tower

The Rookery Building

The Rookery Building is also located in the Loop and was completed in 1888. It is one of Chicago's most significant architectural landmarks. Designed by renowned architects Daniel Burnham and John Wellborn Root, the building originally featured a distinctive red brick and terra cotta façade, which has since been renovated to showcase a stunning glass and iron atrium. Standing at 12 stories tall, the Rookery is notable for being one of the first buildings to use a steel frame, allowing for greater height and more expansive interior spaces. It has been designated a Chicago Landmark and is recognized for its historical significance and innovative design, attracting visitors and architecture enthusiasts alike.

The Aon Center

The Aon Center is located in the heart of Chicago (the Loop). It is a prominent skyscraper that stands at 1,136 feet tall, making it one of the tallest buildings in the city. The building was originally completed as the Standard Oil Building and was rebranded after Aon Corporation acquired naming rights in 2003. It features a unique sloped roof that creates a distinctive silhouette against the Chicago skyline. Interestingly, the Aon Center was once the tallest building in Chicago until it was surpassed by the Willis Tower. The building's elegant white granite exterior is made from the same type of stone used in the construction of the United Nations Headquarters in New York City. The Aon Center also houses a public plaza and artwork, making it not only a hub of business activity but also a vibrant part of Chicago's architectural landscape.

Grant Park

Grant Park is an expansive and historic park that spans over 319 acres in the heart of Chicago's Loop neighborhood. It serves as a vital green space in the bustling downtown area. This urban oasis is home to beautifully landscaped gardens, serene walking paths, and several notable attractions that draw locals and tourists. Among its most famous features is Buckingham Fountain, one of the world's largest and most iconic fountains. Designed by architect Edward H. Bennett and opened in 1927, Buckingham Fountain is inspired by the Latona Fountain at the Palace of Versailles. It is renowned for its impressive water displays, which can shoot water up to 150 feet in the air.

Surrounding the fountain are meticulously maintained gardens that enhance the park's beauty. The fountain becomes even more enchanting at night as it is illuminated with colorful lights, creating a mesmerizing spectacle that captivates onlookers. Grant Park, often referred to as "Chicago's Front Yard," is not only a recreational space but also a cultural hub, hosting various events, concerts, and festivals throughout the year. The park seamlessly connects to the Chicago Lakefront Trail, a scenic 18-mile path that stretches along Lake Michigan and links many of the city's most beloved parks, beaches, and attractions. It's perfect for a leisurely stroll, a scenic bike ride, or simply soaking in the beauty of the city's waterfront.

Buckingham Fountain

Millennium Park

Millennium Park is a vibrant modern park tucked within the larger Grant Park, known for blending cutting-edge art and architecture with lively public spaces. Opened in 2004, it spans 24.5 acres and instantly became one of Chicago's most popular destinations. One of the first things you'll spot is Crown Fountain, where two towering glass block sculptures project video portraits of Chicagoans, and surprise visitors by playfully spouting water. On warm days, kids (and plenty of adults) splash around in the shallow reflecting pool, making it one of the city's favorite summer hangouts. Of course, no trip to Millennium Park is complete without a stop at Cloud Gate, affectionately called "The Bean," where visitors line up to capture its funhouse reflections of the skyline. The park also features the stunning Jay Pritzker Pavilion, designed by Frank Gehry, and ever-changing gardens that burst with seasonal color. Millennium Park perfectly captures Chicago's creative, welcoming spirit year-round with free concerts, public art, outdoor activities, and even winter ice skating.

The Chicago Cultural Center is another must-see, just steps away from Millennium Park. This free public building is home to the world's largest Tiffany stained-glass dome and regularly hosts art exhibits, concerts, and cultural events. With its breathtaking architecture and central location, it's a perfect spot to experience Chicago's rich artistic spirit without spending a dime.

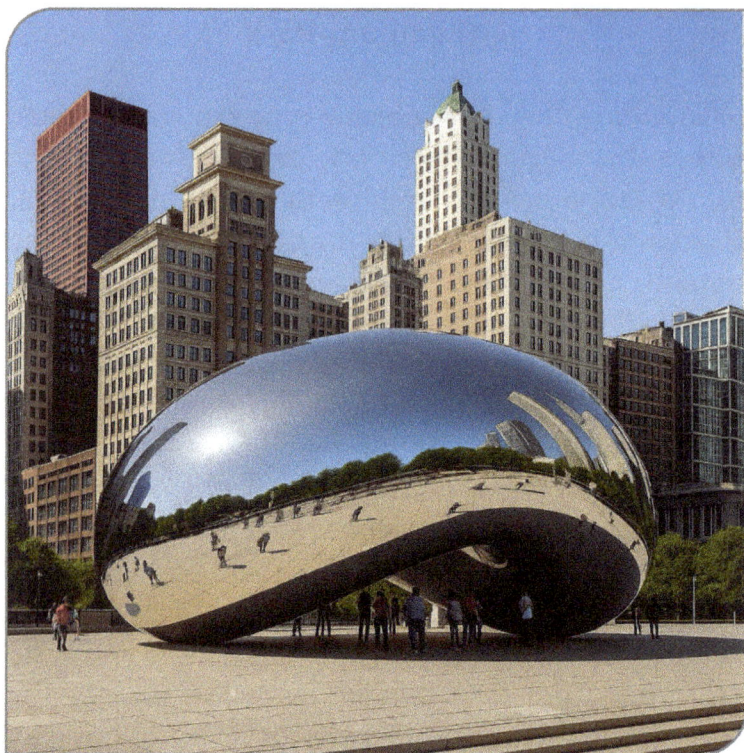

Cloud Gate at Millennium Park (The Bean)

The Lyric Opera House

The Lyric Opera House is located in the Loop neighborhood. It is a stunning venue situated near the downtown area known for its grand architecture and world-class performances. Opened in 1954, the opera house features a striking exterior blending modern and classical design elements, including a stunning lobby showcasing a breathtaking chandelier made of 1,500 crystals. It serves as the home of the

Lyric Opera of Chicago, one of the largest and most respected opera companies in the United States, showcasing a diverse array of operatic productions throughout the year. With a seating capacity of over 3,500, the Lyric Opera House offers exceptional acoustics and a remarkable cultural experience, making it a cherished landmark in the city.

The John Hancock Building

The John Hancock Building, officially known as the John Hancock Center, is an iconic skyscraper located in Chicago's Streeterville neighborhood. Completed in 1970, it rises 1,128 feet and was once the tallest building in the world. Its distinctive X-braced exterior not only gives it a bold, recognizable look but also provides essential structural stability against Chicago's notorious winds. The building houses offices, residences, and the popular 360 CHICAGO observation deck on the 94th floor. Locals know that 360 CHICAGO is a great alternative to the more tourist-heavy Willis Tower Skydeck, offering stunning panoramic views of the city and Lake Michigan without the massive crowds. If you're feeling adventurous, try TILT — a thrilling glass platform that leans outward to give you a heart-pounding view straight down to the streets below. On particularly windy days, you might even feel the building sway slightly, a testament to the innovative engineering that allows it to withstand natural forces. More than just a feat of design, the John Hancock Center remains a proud symbol of Chicago's architectural brilliance and resilience.

The Chicago Water Tower

The Chicago Water Tower is located on the city's Magnificent Mile and was completed in 1869. It is one of the city's most iconic landmarks and a symbol of resilience. Designed by architect William W. Boyington, this stunning Gothic Revival structure stands 154 feet tall and was originally built to house the city's water pumping station. Remarkably, it survived the Great Chicago Fire of 1871, making it one of the few structures to withstand the devastation. The Water Tower is now part of a historic district. It serves as a reminder of Chicago's architectural heritage, attracting visitors who appreciate its historical significance and picturesque design, making it a popular subject for photos.

John Hancock Center and the Chicago Water Tower

Navy Pier

Navy Pier is a popular destination located along the shoreline of Lake Michigan (Streeterville neighborhood). Opening in 1916, it has transformed from a shipping facility into a vibrant entertainment hub, attracting millions of visitors yearly. The pier features a variety of attractions, including the iconic Centennial Wheel, an IMAX theater, and lush gardens, making it a family-friendly destination. The Centennial Wheel (Ferris wheel) at Navy Pier stands at 196 feet tall. It consists of climate-controlled gondolas that offer stunning views of the city and Lake Michigan, making it a must-try experience for visitors. Throughout the year, Navy Pier hosts numerous events and festivals, including live music, cultural celebrations, and seasonal activities like fireworks displays. Firework displays are a highlight during the summer months, usually taking place on Wednesday and Saturday nights (Memorial Day-Labor Day). The fireworks are choreographed to music, creating a stunning experience for viewers. The displays can be seen from various vantage points along the pier and nearby areas, making it a popular destination for families and friends looking to enjoy an evening out. In addition to the traditional summer shows, special fireworks events are often held during holidays and festivals, adding to the festive atmosphere of Navy Pier.

A few more of Navy Pier's attractions include the Chicago Shakespeare Theater and the Chicago Children's Museum. Its beautiful views of the lake and the Chicago skyline provide a picturesque backdrop, making it a favorite spot for locals and tourists.

Navy Pier

Navy Pier offers a variety of boat tours that cater to different interests and preferences. Some of my favorites include The Sea Dog, The Odyssey, and The Tall Ship Windy. The Sea Dog offers a fun and exhilarating experience for visitors looking to explore Lake Michigan and the Chicago skyline. Known for its speed and thrill, the Sea Dog is a high-speed, open-air boat that provides a unique perspective of the city's waterfront. The tour typically includes exciting commentary about Chicago's landmarks and entertaining music. It's a popular choice for families and adventure seekers who want a lively outing on the water, often featuring a splash zone for those looking for an extra thrill. The Odyssey Ship at Navy Pier is a luxurious dining cruise experience that offers impressive views of the Chicago skyline from the water. Guests can enjoy a gourmet meal while cruising along Lake Michigan, with options for brunch, lunch, or firework dinner cruises. The Tall Ship Windy is a stunning 148-foot schooner, offering a unique sailing experience on Lake Michigan. Modeled after the famous sailing vessels of the past, the Windy allows guests to enjoy a leisurely cruise while taking in views of the Chicago skyline and waterfront. During the tour, passengers can learn about the art of sailing and even participate in hoisting the sails. The Windy Ship is especially popular for its sunset cruises, which create a picturesque setting as the sun sets over the lake.

Carbide and Carbon Building

The Carbide and Carbon Building is one of Chicago's most visually distinctive landmarks, known for its dramatic Art Deco design and opulent materials. Another of my favorites, it was completed in 1929 and designed by the Burnham Brothers. The building features a sleek black granite base, dark green terra cotta façade, and is famously topped with a gold-leaf tower and spire, often said to resemble a champagne bottle. Located on Michigan Avenue, this iconic skyscraper originally housed the Union Carbide and Carbon Company and now operates as the Pendry Hotel. Its lavish exterior and historic elegance make it a standout among the city's early 20th-century skyscrapers, adding a touch of glamour to the skyline and a bold example of Jazz Age opulence in architecture.

Carbide and Carbon Building

Tribune Tower

Tribune Tower is located on the Magnificent Mile in Chicago, and is a historic skyscraper known for its stunning neo-Gothic architecture. One of my favorite buildings in the city, it was completed in 1925.

The building was designed to house the Chicago Tribune newspaper and stands at 462 feet tall. The tower's façade features over 140 pieces of stone from famous landmarks worldwide, including fragments from the Colosseum, the Berlin Wall, the Parthenon, the Great Wall of China, and even the Taj Mahal. It was the first building in Chicago to be lit by neon lights when it was completed in 1925. The tower's iconic flying buttresses and intricate carvings make it a prominent feature of Chicago's skyline.

Wrigley Building

The Wrigley Building is just a short 5–10-minute walk from Tribune Tower and was completed in 1924. The building was constructed in 15 months and was the first air-conditioned office building in Chicago, setting a precedent for modern office environments. Known for its distinctive white terra cotta façade and impressive clock tower, the building stands 425 feet tall and blends Renaissance and Gothic architectural styles. The clock tower is modeled after the Giralda of Seville, Spain. Originally built as the headquarters for the Wrigley Company, famous for its chewing gum, the Wrigley Building is situated along the Chicago River, making it a prominent feature of the city's skyline. The structure is also notable for its beautiful nighttime illumination. It is often adorned with seasonal decorations, making it a popular spot for holiday photos and events, which adds to its charm.

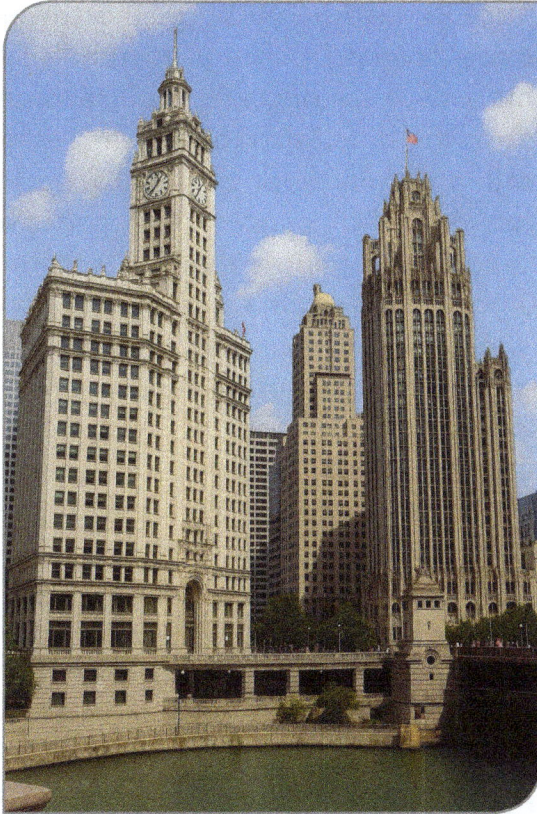

Wrigley Building and Tribune Tower

Marina City

Marina City is a distinctive mixed-use complex located along the Chicago River, not far from the Wrigley Building. Completed in 1964, it consists of two iconic corncob-shaped towers that rise 588 feet and house residential apartments, offices, and a variety of entertainment and dining options. Designed by architect Bertrand Goldberg, the towers were the first residential buildings in the U.S. to be constructed with a concrete shell, a pioneering technique at the time. Each tower features a unique design with a circular floor plan, allowing for stunning views of the Chicago skyline and river. The complex includes a marina that can accommodate up to 60 boats, making it a popular spot for water activities. Additionally, Marina City has appeared in numerous films and television series, reinforcing its reputation as an iconic piece of Chicago's architectural scene. Bertrand Goldberg designed several other notable buildings in Chicago that reflect his innovative approach to architecture. One significant project is the James R. Thompson Center. Others include the River City complex, the Prairie Avenue District and the Dunbar Apartments.

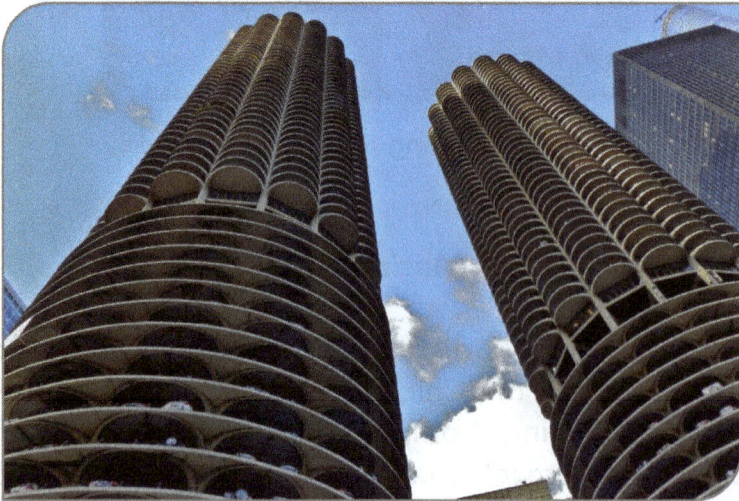

Marina City

The Chicago Merchandise Mart

The Merchandise Mart is one of the largest commercial buildings in the world, spanning over 4.2 million square feet. Opened in 1930, it originally served as a wholesale marketplace for the furniture and interior design industries but has since evolved into a hub for various businesses, including technology and design. The Mart features a distinctive Art Deco architectural style and houses showrooms, offices, and event spaces, making it a vital part of Chicago's commercial landscape. Additionally, the Merchandise Mart is home to Art on the Mart, which is a unique public art installation that transforms the Merchandise Mart into a canvas for digital projections. Launched in 2018, it features large-scale video art displayed on the building's façade, creating a captivating experience for viewers along the Chicago Riverwalk. Art on the Mart occurs year-round, with projections typically shown every evening after sunset. The specific times may vary depending on the season, but the displays are generally visible until around 11 PM. Each season features different curated artworks, making every visit a unique experience. Visitors can enjoy the projections from the Chicago Riverwalk, providing a stunning view of the building's illuminated façade.

Chicago Merchandise Mart

Chicago's Iconic Drawbridges

Massive drawbridges are evident as you explore the city. These captivating bridges not only serve practical purposes, but also enhance the city's skyline with their architectural beauty. These bridges, designed to accommodate both road and river traffic, reflect a rich history of engineering innovation. Visitors can often witness the dramatic process of these bridges raising to allow boats to pass, a sight that captures the unique blend of urban life and waterway navigation that defines Chicago.

Each drawbridge has its own story and character, contributing to the vibrant tapestry of the city's transportation network. When a large vessel needs to pass through, the drawbridges raise vertically creating a dramatic spectacle. The bridges typically raise with schedules, often influenced by maritime traffic and the types of boats navigating the waterways. The raising of the bridges can occur throughout the day but is more common during the warmer months when shipping activity increases. Many bridges have specific schedules that are posted publicly, and the exact times can vary, so boat operators and pedestrians are advised to check local listings or marine traffic apps for real-time updates. The process is usually quick, with each bridge taking only a few minutes to raise and lower, creating a momentary pause in street traffic. It is truly a unique thing to witness!

Visitors can enter certain bridgehouses in Chicago, particularly those that have been converted into visitor centers or museums. For instance, The McCormick Bridgehouse & Chicago River Museum along the Chicago Riverwalk allows guests to explore the history and mechanics of the city's bridges. Inside, you can find exhibits that explain how drawbridges operate and their significance to the city's development. The museum also offers stunning views of the river and the surrounding city, making it a perfect spot for both education and sightseeing. I highly recommend seeing one of these iconic movable bridges in motion, it is a unique and unforgettable Chicago experience.

Chicago Drawbridge

EXPLORING
CHICAGO'S NEIGHBORHOODS

Chicago is a city rich in diversity, and its neighborhoods reflect this vibrant mix of cultures, histories, and lifestyles. Each neighborhood has its own unique character. The South Side features a rich African American heritage, with neighborhoods like Bronzeville showcasing cultural landmarks and a vibrant community spirit. Meanwhile, the Loop serves as the city's central business district, filled with iconic skyscrapers, theaters, and dining options, making it a bustling hub for both work and leisure. Each neighborhood contributes to the city's overall tapestry, making Chicago a dynamic place to live and explore. Chicago's neighborhoods offer something for everyone. With over 200 distinct neighborhoods that make up the 77 community areas in the city of Chicago, it would be nearly impossible to visit them all in one visit. In this guide, we will visit some of the most popular neighborhoods and community areas.

Chicago Community Areas

Chicago's Loop

The Loop is in the heart of the city, known for its iconic skyline, robust arts scene, and rich history. As the central business district, it features a mix of historic architecture and modern skyscrapers, including the famous Willis Tower. This area is home to cultural landmarks such as the Art Institute of Chicago and the Chicago Symphony Orchestra, drawing visitors and locals alike. The Loop is also home to Millennium Park, the Chicago Riverwalk, and some fantastic shopping along State Street. Finally, the Loop is where you will find the Theatre District, always alive with award-winning shows. Stroll the streets and enjoy the glittering marquees of the Cadillac Palace Theatre, the Nederlander Theater, and the Auditorium Theatre. You can't visit the Theater District without snapping a photo under the iconic Chicago Theatre marquee. Sitting proudly on State Street since 1921, this grand old theater is just as stunning inside, with its sweeping staircase and glittering French Baroque-style lobby. Today, the Chicago Theatre hosts everything from concerts to comedy shows, but even if you're not seeing a performance, the sight of those famous lights is practically a rite of passage for anyone visiting the city.

Public transportation is highly accessible, making the Loop a hub for commuters and tourists. Its lively streets are lined with shops, restaurants, and theaters, offering a dynamic urban experience that reflects the essence of Chicago. One of my favorite spots in this area is The London House. Originally built in 1923, it is known for its stunning architecture and prime location along the Chicago River. The hotel features a rooftop bar that offers breathtaking views of the city skyline and the river. I recommend making reservations for the rooftop bar, as it is popular with locals and tourists. The rooftop is transformed during the holidays into Rudolph's Rooftop, which features holiday decor and igloos to keep you warm.

Lincoln Park

Lincoln Park is a vibrant neighborhood located on the North Side of Chicago. It is home to several popular tourist attractions, making it a must-see destination in Chicago. One of the main highlights is the Lincoln Park Zoo, which offers free admission and features a diverse range of animals in a beautiful setting. Nearby, the Lincoln Park Conservatory showcases stunning plant collections and themed gardens, providing a serene escape within the city. The neighborhood also includes the picturesque Lincoln Park itself, where visitors can enjoy walking paths, picnic areas, and views of the Chicago skyline. Additionally, attractions like the Chicago History Museum, which offers engaging exhibits on the city's past, and various theaters and cultural venues contribute to the vibrant atmosphere of Lincoln Park. Its blend of nature, culture, and urban living adds to Lincoln Park's reputation as one of Chicago's most desirable neighborhoods.

Make sure to stop by Kingston Mines and listen to some legendary Chicago-style blues. This neighborhood is also a shopper's delight. You will find a vast number of beautiful boutiques and unique décor. If you work up an appetite, enjoy waterfront views at the Lakefront Restaurant. Other options include Café Ba-Ba-Reeba, Geja's Café (fondue), and Michelin-starred Boka. If you're looking for a classic Chicago beach day with postcard-worthy skyline views, head to North Avenue Beach. Located along the Lakefront Trail near Lincoln Park. It's a popular spot for volleyball tournaments, sunbathing, swimming, and people-watching. The beach also features a distinctive beach house designed to look like an ocean liner and plenty of snack stands, bike rentals, and watersport options. It's one of the best places to take in both Lake Michigan and the city skyline at once.

Lakeview

Lakeview is a lively neighborhood also located on the north side of Chicago, known for its fun atmosphere and diverse community. One of its most notable attractions is Wrigley Field, the historic home of the Chicago Cubs, which draws baseball fans from all over. Wrigley Field is one of the most iconic baseball stadiums in the United States and boasts a rich history dating back to its opening in 1914. Boystown, located in the Lakeview area, is renowned as one of the oldest and most vibrant LGBTQ+ districts in the United States. Known for its colorful pride-themed decorations and welcoming atmosphere, Boystown boasts a lively nightlife scene with numerous bars, clubs, and restaurants catering to diverse tastes. The area is also famous for hosting the annual Chicago Pride Parade, which attracts thousands of participants and spectators annually.

The Lakeview area is also home to the Lakeview East Festival of the Arts, typically held in September. Belmont Harbor is a picturesque harbor, perfect for boating, or walking along the shoreline and taking in the views of Lake Michigan. The Music Box Theatre is a historic cinema known for its independent films, classic movies, and unique screenings. Other notable attractions include the Mercury Theater and the Laugh Factory. For a casual bite, DryHop Brewers is a popular stop for house-made beer and bites. Also, try BITES Asian Kitchen, which serves up sushi, ramen, and Asian-inspired tapas, or El Mariachi, known for its fun atmosphere and fantastic margaritas. Dear Margaret has earned Michelin acclaim for its French-Canadian cuisine, and Coda di Volpe offers southern Italian fare paired with neighborhood charm.

Old Town

Old Town spans parts of two official community areas: Lincoln Park and the Near North Side. It is a historic neighborhood known for its charming streets, vibrant culture, and rich architectural heritage. It is the birthplace of modern American improv. Second City is a renowned improv and sketch comedy theater that has played a pivotal role in shaping the landscape of American comedy. Founded in 1959, it has become a launching pad for many famous comedians, actors, and writers, including the likes of Bill Murray, Chevy Chase, Gilda Radner, Aidy Bryant, Mike Myers, Chris Farley, Key & Peele, John Belushi, Tina Fey, and Steve Carell, among others. Once a hub for bohemian artists and musicians, it has transformed into a trendy area filled with boutique shops, restaurants, and nightlife spots.

Each year in June, the Old Town Art Fair brings over 200 nationally acclaimed artists together to showcase their work, drawing a crowd of 30,000 art lovers. Visitors can also explore the Old Town Triangle Historic District, which showcases beautiful Victorian-era homes. With its blend of history and modernity, Old Town offers a unique atmosphere that attracts both locals and tourists alike. While in Old Town, grab some ribs at Twin Anchors, a former speakeasy where Frank Sinatra was a regular. You can also sip a glass of wine at the House of Glunz, Chicago's oldest wine merchant (setting up shop over 120 years ago). The Old Town Ale House is another local watering hole, a favorite of Anthony Bourdain. If you have a sweet tooth, stop by the Fudge Pot, where everything has been made in-store since 1963.

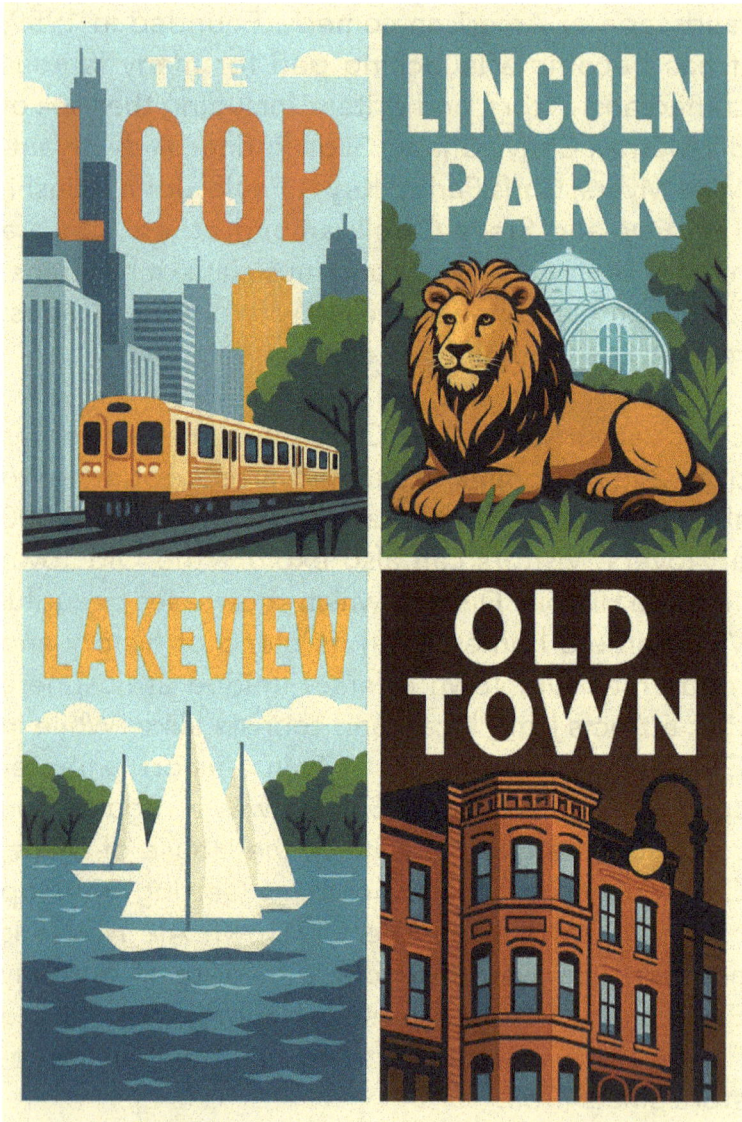

The Loop, Lincoln Park, Lakeview, Old Town

Chicago's Gold Coast

The Gold Coast neighborhood, located within the Near North Side community area, is a prestigious area known for its luxurious residences, historic buildings, and upscale shopping. Nestled along Lake Michigan, it boasts beautiful tree-lined streets and is home to some of the city's wealthiest residents. The neighborhood features an array of high-end boutiques, fine dining establishments, and vibrant nightlife options. Landmarks such as the historic Water Tower and the famous Oak Street Beach exemplify the area's charm and appeal. With its blend of opulence and cultural attractions, the Gold Coast remains one of Chicago's most desirable neighborhoods. Restaurants favored by both past and present celebrities help give this neighborhood its star power.

The Gold Coast boasts several architectural treasures, including the Astor Street District, the Charnley-Persky House (a collaboration between Louis Sullivan and Frank Lloyd Wright), and the historic Playboy Mansion. This neighborhood is also home to the International Museum of Surgical Science, one of the most unique museums in the country. If you have the time, you can catch a show at the Porchlight Music Theater, visit the Newberry Library, or dine in the lovely courtyard of a historic building at the 3 Arts Club Café. One of my favorite places to dine is Maple & Ash. This restaurant is celebrated for its contemporary take on classic steakhouse fare. With its commitment to excellence and a focus on hospitality, Maple & Ash is a must-visit for food enthusiasts. Adalina (a Michelin-starred restaurant) is another stylish and contemporary restaurant located on the Gold Coast, known for its vibrant atmosphere and innovative cuisine. It's often named one of the world's best restaurants, focusing on seasonal and locally sourced ingredients. I also recommend stopping in Sparrow, located on Elm Street. It is housed in a restored 1927 Ard Deco apartment building and offers a cozy vintage atmosphere. The bar specializes in rum-focused cocktails and features a curated selection of spirits, wines, and beers. Please note that Sparrow does not serve food and operates on a walk-in basis, as they do not accept reservations.

River North

River North is a dynamic neighborhood known for its vibrant arts scene, upscale dining, and lively nightlife. Located just north of the Chicago River, in the Near North Side, this area is home to a concentration of art galleries, including the renowned Merchandise Mart, which showcases contemporary design and architecture. River North boasts a variety of restaurants, from casual eateries to fine dining establishments, making it a popular destination for food lovers. The neighborhood's lively atmosphere is complemented by its proximity to the Magnificent Mile, offering shopping and entertainment options that attract both locals and visitors. This neigh-borhood is home to some of the hottest nightlife scenes, where you can keep the party going until the early morning hours. With its mix of culture, cuisine, and convenience, River North stands out as one of Chicago's most desirable areas.

River North offers an endless list of dining options; I am going to touch on a few of my favorites. The Tortoise Supper Club is known for its upscale yet comfortable atmosphere and menu that highlights classic American fare with a contemporary twist. The Tortoise Supper Club often features live music, making it a popular spot for locals and visitors look-ing for a fun night out. Tao Chicago is located in a historic building that has seen various transforma-tions over the years, often leading to speculation about its haunted status. Being a former theater, the building itself has a rich history that could con-tribute to ghostly tales. Patrons sometimes share reports of unusual occurrences, such as unexplained sounds or feelings of being watched, which add to the restaurant's mysterious charm. Whether or not it is truly haunted, the combination of its vibrant atmosphere and historical significance makes it an intriguing destination. Other incredible options include River Roast, RPM Steak and RPM Seafood, Gene & Georgetti's, Frontera Grill, and Gibson's Italia. This upscale Italian steakhouse offers stunning views of the Chicago River and the city skyline. For a fun night out, I recommend dinner at Havana and an after-dinner stop at Three Dots and a Dash. Havana is known for its lively atmosphere and Cuban-inspired cuisine, while Three Dots and a Dash is a popular tiki bar showcasing an extensive selection of rum-based cocktails, many of which are crafted with house-made syrups and fresh ingredients. Three Dots and a Dash can be tricky to find; head to 435 N Clark Street. The entrance is somewhat discreet, located in an alleyway, adding to its secretive tiki vibe.

Streeterville

Streeterville is situated along the picturesque shoreline of Lake Michigan and is part of the Near North Side community area. Known for its stunning skyline views and proximity to the Magnificent Mile, Streeterville boasts a lively mix of residential, commercial, and recreational spaces. Major attractions include Navy Pier, with its entertainment options and events, and the renowned Museum of Contemporary Art. The area is also home to upscale hotels, fine dining establishments, and a bustling nightlife scene, making it a popular destination for both tourists and locals. Streeterville is a key part of Chicago's urban landscape with its blend of culture, entertainment, and scenic beauty. There are plenty of dining options at Navy Pier, but why not get a bite to eat and play a round of indoor bocce ball at Pinstripes? If you time it right, you can even watch the fireworks from their outdoor patio.

Art lovers shouldn't miss the Museum of Contemporary Art (MCA), which is just steps from the Magnificent Mile in Streeterville. One of the most prominent contemporary art museums in the United States, the MCA showcases an ever-evolving mix of visual arts, design, performance, and film. Whether you're interested in avant-garde installations or thought-provoking exhibits, the MCA offers a cutting-edge window into the world of modern creativity, all housed in a sleek, modernist building designed by architect Josef Paul Kleihues.

Uptown

The Uptown neighborhood is celebrated for its rich history, cultural diversity, and vibrant arts scene. Once a center for jazz and blues, it now showcases a blend of historic architecture, parks, and a variety of community events. This area boasts a long-standing legacy as an entertainment hub, featuring an eclectic mix of restaurants, shops, and venues that embody its multicultural essence. Vintage theaters and classic jazz clubs coexist with a dynamic selection of international cuisine. Key landmarks include the Aragon Ballroom and the Uptown Theatre. Local favorites range from authentic African dishes at Demera Ethiopian Restaurant to live performances at the Black Ensemble Theater, and relaxing spots like Montrose Beach and Crema Coffee Shop. Uptown thrived with nightlife during the 1920s and 1930s, highlighted by the iconic Green Mill, a jazz club that retains the sultry ambiance of its Prohibition-era past, famously frequented by gangster Al Capone. Nearby, the Baton Show Lounge has been a renowned drag venue for over 50 years, offering nightly live shows. For country music fans, Carol's Pub is a must-visit for live performances. The Argyle Street area is a culinary gem for Asian cuisine, featuring sushi, dim sum, banh mi, and pho.

Other popular spots include James Beard Award-winning Sun Wah BBQ, known for its Beijing duck dinner, and Pho Viet for traditional Vietnamese dishes. In the summer, the Argyle Night Market comes alive with vendors, entertainment, and cultural performances, while winter brings the vibrant Argyle Lunar New Year celebration, including a colorful parade. For a beach experience that feels a little more local, head to Montrose Beach. Known for its expansive sandy shoreline, casual vibe, and panoramic skyline views, Montrose Beach is a favorite for families, dog owners, and birdwatchers alike. It's less crowded than beaches closer to downtown and offers beautiful green spaces nearby, including the Montrose Point Bird Sanctuary and a scenic harbor.

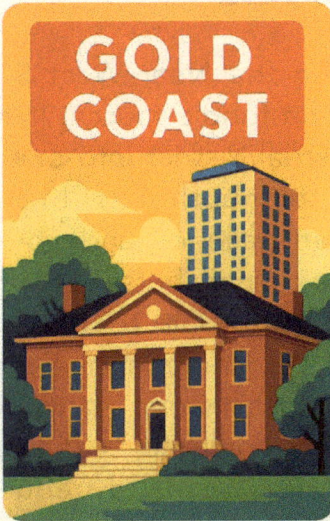

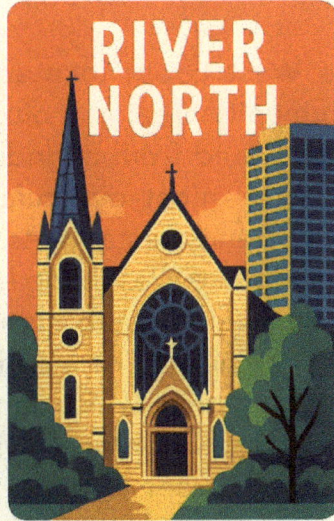

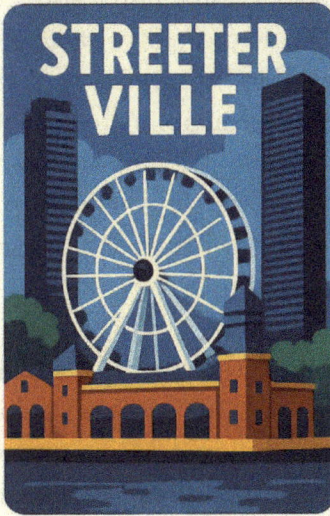

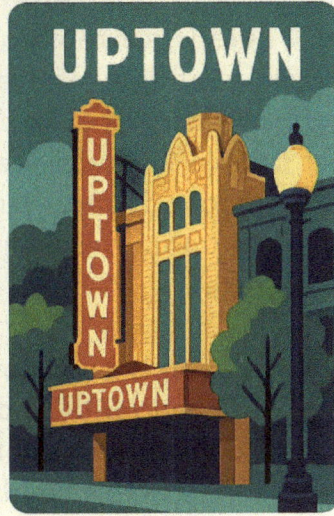

Gold Coast, River North, Streeterville, Uptown

The West Loop

The West Loop, located in the Near West Side community area, is a bit of a foodie mecca. It has transformed from an industrial district into one of the city's most dynamic neighborhoods. Known for its trendy restaurants, art galleries, and vibrant nightlife, the West Loop is a culinary hotspot featuring renowned establishments like Girl & The Goat and Au Cheval. The area is also home to the Fulton Market District, which combines historic charm with modern development. Visitors can enjoy the picturesque streets, unique boutiques, and frequent pop-up events that showcase local talent and culture. There is a stretch of Randolph Street known as Restaurant Row, where you will find many of the neighborhood's most celebrated spots. A few of the most popular include Green Street Smoked Meats (house-smoked barbecue), Avec (creative small plates), Momotaro (sushi), and Monteverde (freshly made pasta).

The West Loop is also home to Greektown, a vibrant area overflowing with traditional restaurants, bakeries, and delis. The National Hellenic Museum can also be found in this neighborhood. It is the second oldest American institution dedicated to Greek culture. Nearby Fulton Market, with its industrial vibe, has additional trendy shops and restaurants to visit. Some notable spots to visit are Time Out Market, Aba, and The Publican. The Epiphany Center for the Arts is a former church that now hosts rotating exhibits, live music, and performing arts. The year-round Randolph Street Market is a great place for unusual vintage and antique finds.

Little Italy

Little Italy, also located in the Near West Side community area, is a neighborhood steeped in Italian heritage and culture. Known for its delicious restaurants, bustling markets, and charming streets, Little Italy offers a taste of Italy in the heart of the city. The area is home to several historic landmarks, including the University of Illinois at Chicago and the iconic Taylor Street, often referred to as the heart of the neighborhood. Visitors can enjoy authentic Italian cuisine, local festivals, and a warm community atmosphere that reflects its rich immigrant history. To get your fill of Italian cuisine, check out The Rosebud, Tufano's Vernon Park Tap (a James Beard Award winner), Pompei (family-owned for four generations), and in the summer, make sure to stop at Mario's Italian Lemonade. Other attractions include Jane Addams Hull House Museum, The Shrine of Our Lady of Pompeii, and the Notre Dame de Chicago. There are also many churches and Italian architectural structures, such as the John Coughlan House built in 1871, Saint Basil, and Holy Family.

Pilsen

Pilsen, located in the Lower West Side community area, is known for its rich Mexican heritage and artistic community. The area is famous for its colorful murals that adorn many buildings, showcasing the work of local artists and reflecting cultural themes. Pilsen is also home to a variety of traditional Mexican restaurants, bakeries, and shops, making it a culinary destination. The neighborhood hosts several cultural events throughout the year, including the Pilsen Mexican Independence Day Parade, which celebrates the community's heritage and unity. It was named one of the coolest neighborhoods around the world by Forbes. The thriving art scene has become known as the Chicago Arts District. It consists of a seven-block stretch filled with artist lofts, studios, retail spaces, galleries, and more.

The Pilsen Arts and Community House is another must-see for art lovers. Stop by the Museum of Mexican Art while here; the free museum immerses visitors in Mexican culture. Some notable eateries include HaiSous (Vietnamese), 5 Rabanitos (Mexican staples), S.K.Y (globally inspired flavors), and Punch House (70's vibes and large format drinks). You can't leave without exploring the music venue, Thalia Hall. You can catch indie rockers, comedians, DJs, and more in a venue modeled after the Prague Opera House. It shares a historic building with Punch House and Tack Room (live piano music). Additionally, Pilsen hosts events like the 18th Street Pilsen

Art Walk, where residents and tourists can engage with local artists and experience the cultural tapestry of this unique Chicago neighborhood.

Little Village

Little Village, often referred to as "La Villita," is a lively neighborhood in Chicago that serves as a hub for the Mexican community. It is in the South Lawndale community area and is known for its vibrant culture. The area boasts a plethora of authentic Mexican restaurants, bakeries, and shops that reflect its rich heritage. The neighborhood is also famous for its annual events, such as the Little Village Mexican Independence Day Parade, which draws large crowds and showcases traditional music, dance, and cuisine.

With colorful murals and a strong sense of community, Little Village offers a unique blend of culture and tradition in the heart of Chicago. Wander 26th Street, the neighborhood's main drag and one of the busiest shopping districts in Chicago. It is a two-mile stretch that is home to close to 500 businesses. Some notable eateries include El Milagro (fresh tortillas made in-house), Nuevo Leon (casual Mexican classics), Mi Tierra (fantastic margaritas) and Yolanda's Restaurant (handmade recipes 24 hours a day). You can also pick up a treat from a paletero selling frozen treats (a pushcart vendor). Olsito's Tap is a speakeasy-style bar, while La Cueva is an LGBTQ+ nightclub known as the oldest Latino drag bar in the country.

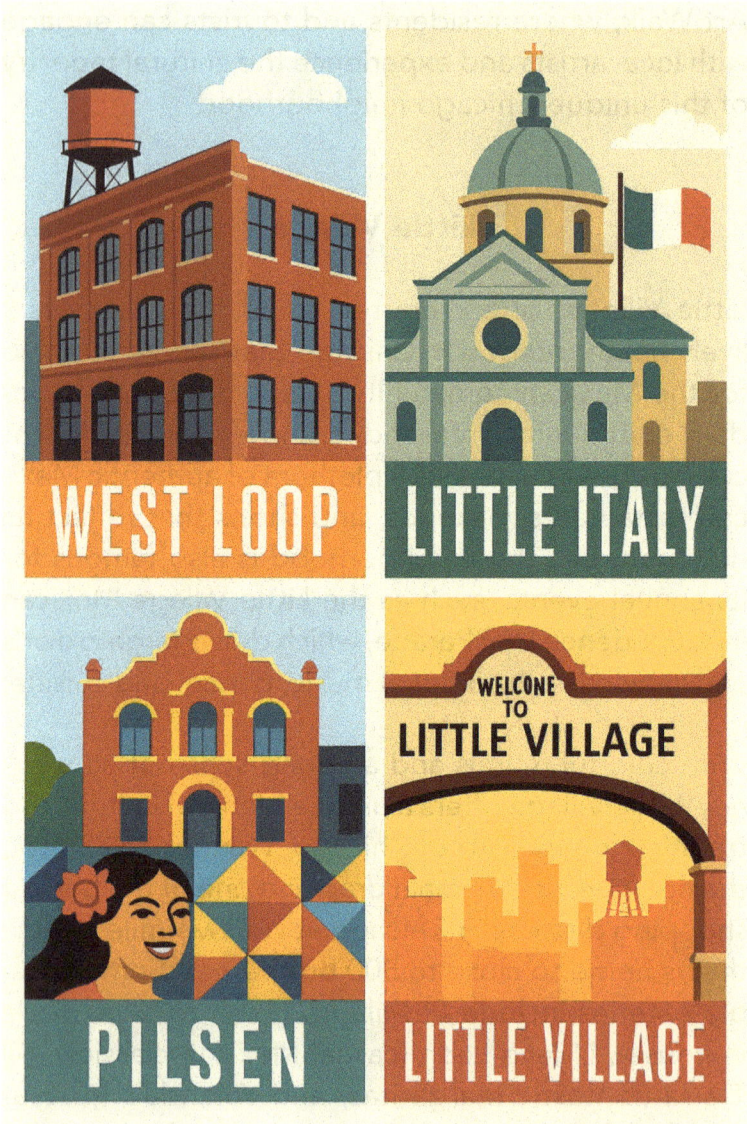

West Loop, Little Italy, Pilsen, Little Village

Wicker Park

Wicker Park, located in West Town, is known for its eclectic mix of culture, art, and nightlife. Once a hub for Polish immigrants, it has transformed into a trendy area filled with boutiques, galleries, and hip restaurants. The centerpiece of Wicker Park is the park itself, offering green space for relaxation and community events. For an elevated urban adventure, check out the 606 Trail. Once an abandoned rail line, the 606 has been transformed into a 2.7-mile-long elevated greenway and park system, connecting several northwest side neighborhoods like Wicker Park, Bucktown, and Logan Square. It's a favorite for walkers, runners, and cyclists, offering a unique perspective on Chicago's diverse residential areas, plus lots of public art and garden spaces along the way.

The lively Six Corners area, where North, Milwaukee, and Damen Avenues converge, serves as the vibrant core of the neighborhood. It is home to a variety of vintage shops, record stores, noodle restaurants, award-winning dining spots, trendy coffee shops, bookstores, art galleries, and much more, creating a dynamic atmosphere. This area is also famous for its historic architecture and as a focal point for Chicago's music scene, making it a must-visit destination for both locals and tourists alike. Try an artisanal drink at The Violet Hour, catch a show at Subterranean (a music venue in a century-old industrial building), and visit the rooftop bar in the Robey Hotel to take in some panoramic views of the skyline. Wicker Park is known for some exceptional dining. Some local favorites include Tex-Mex brunch at Dove's Luncheonette, Italian fare at Club Lucky, unique plant dishes at Bloom, award-winning French cuisine at Pompette, and classic New Orleans po'boys at Ina Mae Tavern. This area is also home to some of the city's best indie music venues, late-night clubs, pubs, and dive bars.

Bronzeville

Bronzeville, located in the Douglas and Grand Boulevard community areas on the South Side of Chicago, is a historic neighborhood renowned for its rich African American heritage and cultural significance. Once a thriving center of African American life, Bronzeville is home to iconic landmarks like the Victory Monument and the historic Chicago Defender Building. The area boasts a vibrant arts scene, with numerous galleries and theaters showcasing local talent. One of the most well-known events that takes place in Bronzeville is the annual Bud Billiken Parade, the nation's largest African-American parade, which draws more than one million spectators each August. While in Bronzeville, take the Bronzeville Art District Tour and visit Gallery Guichard, Faie African Art Gallery, and the Bronzeville Artist Lofts. This community is celebrated for its deep historical roots and a thriving contemporary revival. Bronzeville has made significant cultural contributions, having been the home of notable figures such as Pulitzer Prize-winning poet Gwendolyn Brooks, and civil rights pioneer Ida B. Wells. Be sure to visit the Robert W. Roloson Houses, the only row homes ever constructed by Frank Lloyd Wright.

As you explore, take a moment to admire the former homes of iconic entertainers such as Louis Armstrong, Nat King Cole, and the Marx Brothers, along with trailblazers like Bessie Coleman, who was the first African American woman to earn a pilot's license. Amidst all this rich history, be sure to seek out unique public art pieces, including a sculpture-lined section of Martin Luther King Drive that showcases the Monument to the Great Migration, the Bronzeville Walk of Fame, and The Victory Monument. Additionally, the Ida B. Wells Monument is located just a few blocks from her former home. If you get hungry and want to get a bite to eat, stop by Truth Italian (soulful take on classic Italian), Pearl's Place (Southern soul food), Norman's Bistro (Sunday jazz), Pier 31 (lakefront views) or the Bronzeville Winery (patio and live music).

Chinatown

Chinatown, located in Armour Square, showcases the rich culture and heritage of the Chinese community. Known for its colorful storefronts, authentic restaurants, and bustling markets, Chinatown offers a unique blend of traditional and contemporary Chinese experiences. Visitors can explore landmarks such as the Chinatown Gate, which serves as a welcoming entrance, and the Chinese-American Museum of Chicago, which highlights the contributions of Chinese immigrants. The area is particularly lively during festivals like the Chinese New Year, when the streets come alive with parades, lion dances, and cultural performances, making it a must-visit destination for both locals and tourists. Make sure to see the Nine Dragon Wall, which is a jewel-toned piece of art that honors ancient Chinese folklore. Try some authentic Chinese sweets at Autea Sweets and Eats or Chiu Quon (the neighborhood's oldest bakery). There is no shortage of fantastic places to eat. Some include Strings Ramen, Evergreen Restaurant (Cantonese specialties), and Ming Hin. A few other things to see in Chinatown include the Pui Tak Center, the ART Gallery, Chinatown Square, and the Ping Tom Memorial Park.

The South Loop

The South Loop, mainly located within the Near South Side community area, is an energetic neighborhood celebrated for its rich history and contemporary development. Once primarily an industrial zone, it has evolved into a lively hub that features a blend of residential, commercial, and cultural spaces. Key attractions in the South Loop include the Field Museum, the Shedd Aquarium, and the Adler Planetarium (the Museum Campus), all situated along the picturesque lakefront. The area also boasts a burgeoning dining scene, trendy boutiques, and convenient access to public transportation.

Enjoy a performance at Buddy Guy's Legends, where the legendary musician takes the stage each January. Take a tour of Chess Records, the historic site where many blues legends recorded their timeless hits. For beer enthusiasts, Moody Tongue offers the unique experience of being the world's only Michelin-starred brewery. To indulge your sweet tooth, head to Decadent for a delightful selection of treats. Explore the historic Motor Row District, Chicago's former automobile manufacturing center, which has transformed into an entertainment hotspot featuring the vibrant Lips Drag Palace, VU Rooftop bar, Duneyrr Fermenta brewery, and more. In the adjacent Prairie Avenue District, stroll along "Millionaire's Row," lined with opulent mansions that once belonged to the city's elite, including the historic Glessner House museum. Additionally, the South Loop is home to Soldier Field, making it a favored destination for Bears fans during the fall and winter months.

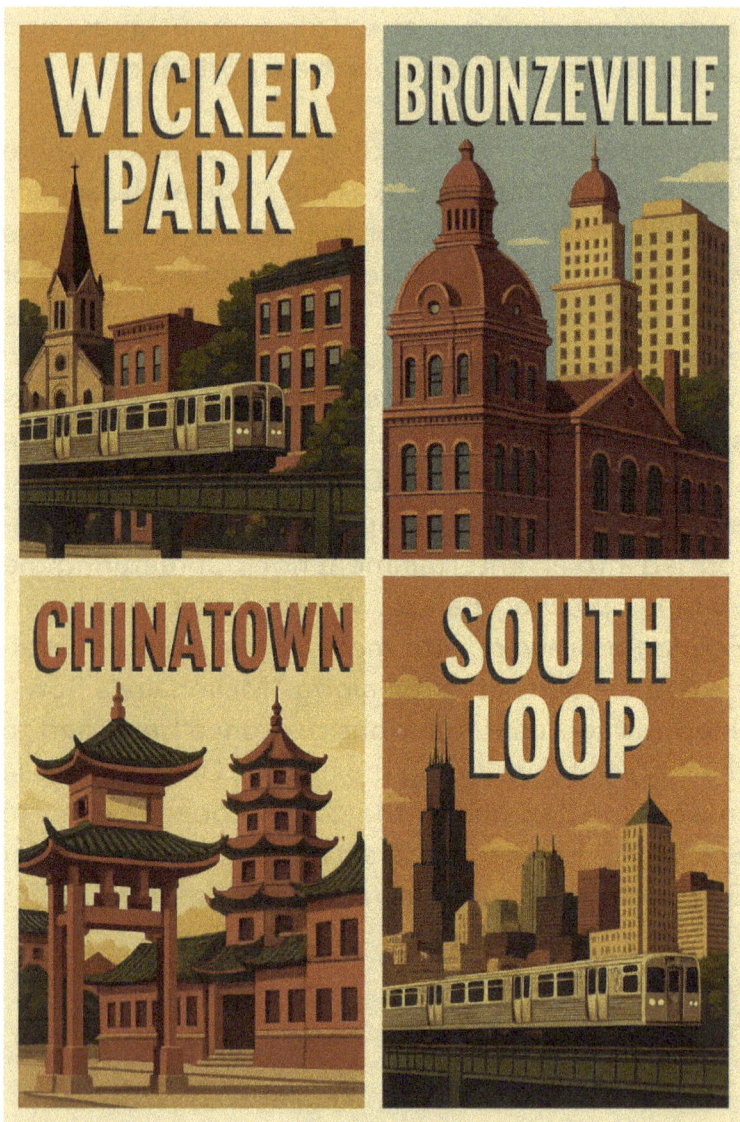

Wicker Park, Bronzeville, Chinatown, South Loop

Hyde Park

Hyde Park is a diverse and historic neighborhood located on the South Side of Chicago, renowned for its cultural institutions and vibrant community. Home to the prestigious University of Chicago, the area boasts stunning architecture, including the iconic Robie House designed by Frank Lloyd Wright. Hyde Park is also known for its beautiful parks, such as Washington Park and Jackson Park, which offer ample green space for outdoor activities. Don't miss a visit to Promontory Point, a beautiful man-made peninsula extending into Lake Michigan. It is known for its panoramic views of the Chicago skyline and peaceful lakefront setting, and it's a favorite spot for picnicking, swimming, and watching the sunrise or sunset.

Hyde Park also hosts a variety of shops, restaurants, and cultural events, making it a lively destination for both residents and visitors. Hyde Park was the site of the Chicago World's Fair of 1893 and home to former President Barack Obama. Some of the highlights you don't want to miss in Hyde Park are the Museum of Science and Industry, the architecture of the University of Chicago, Frank Lloyd Wright's Robie House, DuSable Black History Museum, The Fountain of Time, the Hyde Park Art Center, Osaka Garden, and Promontory Point. If you are hungry, you can grab breakfast at Valois Restaurant, a favorite of Barack Obama.

The Magnificent Mile

The Magnificent Mile may not a neighborhood or community area, but it is worth mentioning. The Mag Mile is a renowned stretch of Michigan Avenue located within the Near North Side, celebrated for its luxurious shopping, dining, and entertainment options. Spanning from the Chicago River to Oak Street, this vibrant avenue is lined with iconic sky-scrapers, historic landmarks, and upscale boutiques, making it a popular destination. The area boasts an impressive mix of high-end retailers, department stores, fine dining establishments, and cultural attractions such as the Art Institute of Chicago and the historic Water Tower.

The Magnificent Mile is also known for its stunning architecture, featuring a blend of modern skyscrap-ers and classic buildings, creating a unique urban landscape that reflects Chicago's architectural heri-tage. If you are an American Girl fan, check out Water Tower Place. One of the highlights is the Doll Hair Salon, where visitors can get their dolls styled, and the Café, which provides a charming setting to enjoy a meal. Another popular destination on the Mag-nificent Mile is the world's largest Starbucks. This flagship store, which opened in November 2019, spans over 35,000 square feet and features mul-tiple levels, offering a unique experience for coffee lovers. Events such as the Magnificent Mile Lights Festival further enhance this area's appeal, drawing crowds to experience the festive atmosphere of this bustling thoroughfare.

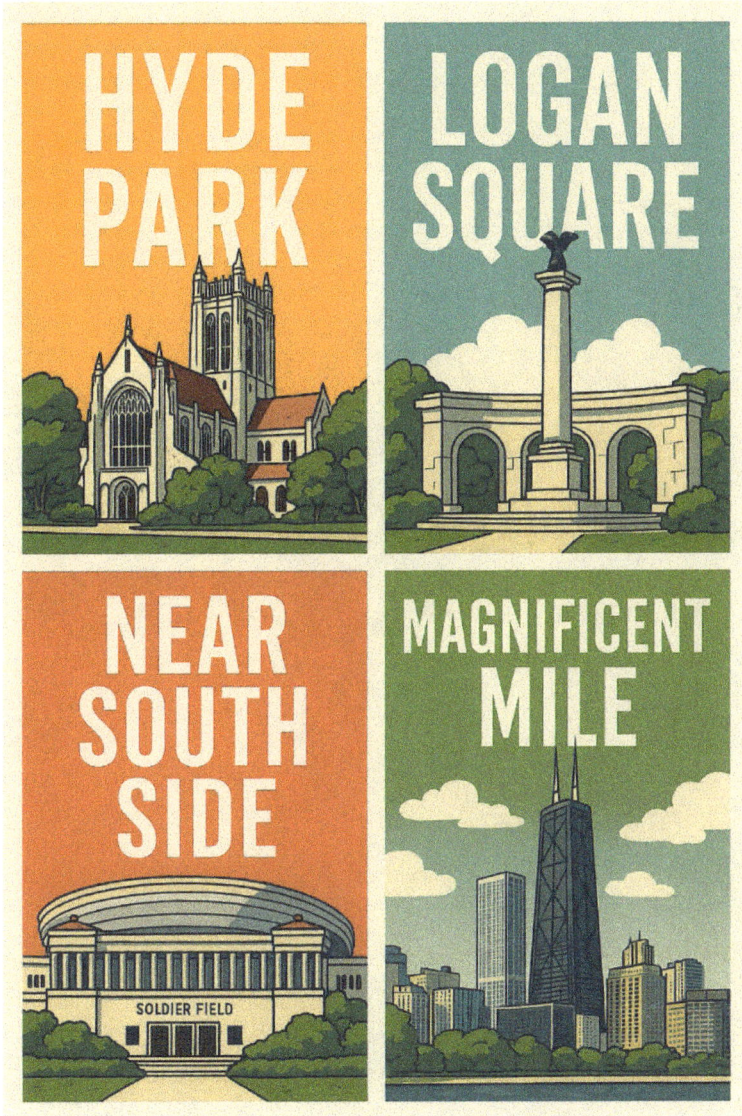

Hyde Park, Logan Square, Near South Side, Magnificent Mile

GETTING AROUND CHICAGO

Chicago offers a variety of transportation options, making it easy for residents and visitors to navigate the city efficiently. The Chicago Transit Authority (CTA) operates an extensive network of buses and trains, including the iconic "L" trains that provide rapid access to various neighborhoods and attractions. For those who prefer to drive, the city has a well-maintained road system, though traffic can be congested during peak hours. Biking is also popular, with numerous bike lanes and the Divvy bike-sharing program available for convenient rentals. Additionally, the Chicago Water Taxi offers a scenic way to travel along the river, connecting key areas while providing stunning views of the city skyline. Taxis and rideshare services like Uber and Lyft provide flexible options for quick trips. With these diverse modes of transportation, getting around Chicago is both practical and enjoyable. We will take a closer look at several of the different ways to get around the city.

When exploring the city, I highly recommend taking advantage of one of the Chicago River cruises. Chicago offers a variety of river tours that cater to different interests. Popular options include the Architecture River Cruise, which focuses on the city's

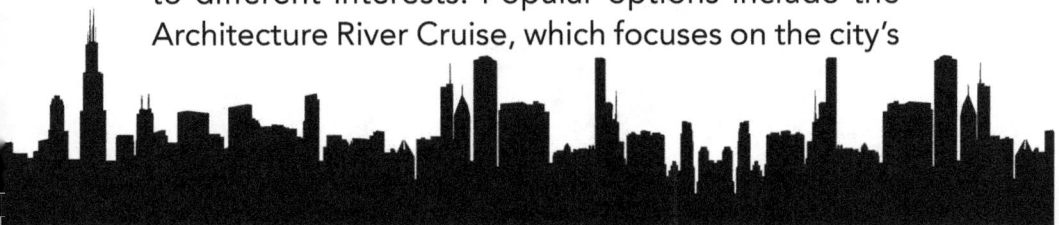

iconic buildings and their history; the Chicago River History Tour, which delves into the river's significance in the city's development; and the Fireworks Cruise, which combines stunning views of the skyline with a fireworks display. Additionally, there are specialty tours, such as the Chicago River Kayak Tours for a more hands-on experience, and themed cruises, such as those featuring live music or dining experiences. These tours offer a unique perspective on the City's amazing architecture and rich history and are popular among tourists and locals alike. Nothing beats a boat ride down the Chicago River on a beautiful day!

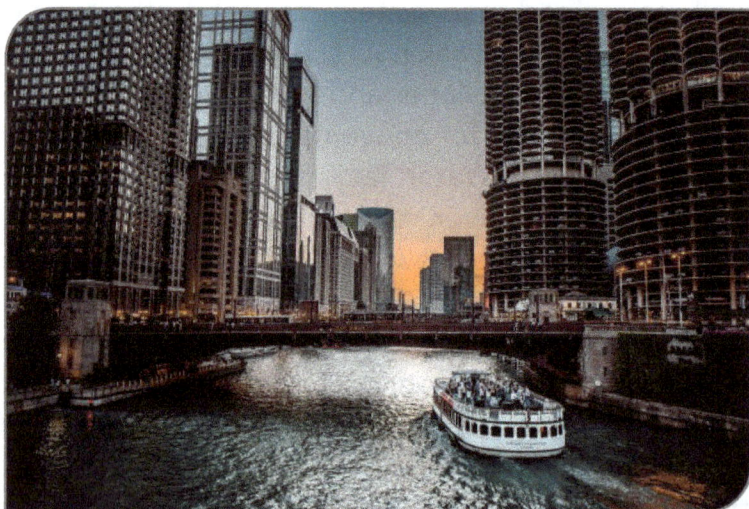

Chicago River Tour

The Chicago Water Taxi is a distinctive transportation service that operates along the Chicago River, offering a delightful and scenic alternative to traditional land-based transport. This service connects various neighborhoods and key attractions, including the bustling Loop, the trendy River North area, and the vibrant Chinatown, making it an efficient way to navigate the city. With multiple boarding points, riders can embark on a leisurely journey while taking in breathtaking views of Chicago's iconic skyline and architectural marvels. Each ride provides a unique perspective of the city, allowing passengers to appreciate the blend of urban life and natural beauty. The Water Taxi experience is particularly popular during warm months, as it provides both a practical means of transport and a memorable way to enjoy the sights and sounds of Chicago from the water, attracting both locals and visitors alike.

Chicago Water Taxi

The Chicago Big Bus Tour is a popular and enjoyable way to discover the city's iconic landmarks and attractions while seated comfortably on an open-top double-decker bus. This tour offers multiple routes that cover a wide array of Chicago's historical and cultural landmarks, providing a comprehensive overview of the city's architecture and rich history.

Knowledgeable guides deliver live commentary, sharing fascinating stories and insights about the sites along the route, from the stunning Art Deco buildings to the historic neighborhoods. One of the tour's standout features is the hop-on, hop-off option, allowing passengers to disembark at various stops to explore specific attractions, such as Millennium Park, the Art Institute of Chicago, or Navy Pier, at their own pace. This flexibility, combined with the unique vantage point from the bus, makes the Chicago Big Bus Tour a favorite choice for both tourists and locals looking to experience the city in a relaxed and informative way.

The Chicago Riverwalk is a scenic pathway along the Chicago River that offers a unique perspective of the city's architecture and vibrant waterfront. Stretching approximately 1.25 miles, the Riverwalk features picturesque views, public art installations, and a variety of dining options, making it a popular destination. Whether you're in the mood to relax, party it up, or soak in some culture, the Riverwalk offers something for everyone. It also offers excellent views of the largest video-projected artwork in the world, Art on the Mart, transforming the Merchandise Mart into a canvas for digital projections.

The Chicago Riverwalk

As I mentioned earlier, the Chicago 606 is an innovative elevated park and trail system that repurposes an old rail line into a multi-use path for pedestrians and cyclists. Stretching approximately 2.7 miles, the 606 connects several neighborhoods, including Logan Square, Humboldt Park, and Wicker Park. It offers a scenic route adorned with art installations, greenery, and community spaces. The 606 provides a recreational area for outdoor activities while promoting connectivity between neighborhoods, making it a popular destination for everyone.

Chicago's CTA "L" Rail System

Utilizing the Chicago Transit Authority (CTA) is an excellent way to discover the city's varied neighborhoods. You can begin by acquiring a Ventra card, which serves as a transit pass for both trains and buses. Ventra cards are available for purchase at vending machines in train stations, certain retail outlets, online, or via the app. After obtaining your card, you can load it with money or buy a pass for unlimited rides for a given duration. To navigate the CTA system effectively, consider downloading the CTA app or visiting their website for real-time updates on train and bus routes, schedules, and service alerts. The CTA features several train lines identified by color (such as the Red Line and Blue Line), with train maps available at stations and online. These train lines are often referred to as "the L," which stands for "elevated." This nickname comes from the trains that run on elevated tracks above the streets of the city. Key stops include downtown regions like the Loop, where many attractions can be found. Buses complement the train system by serving neighborhoods not directly accessible by train. Bus stops display route numbers and schedules, and you can track them in real time using the CTA app. Transfers between buses and trains are free when using a Ventra card. Familiarizing yourself with the train and bus route maps will simplify your trip planning. Always check the CTA website or app for the latest service alerts regarding delays or changes. Download the CTA app for real-time arrival updates, route planning, and fare management. Knowing the landmarks and attractions near your destination can also help with navigation.

Hidden just beneath the bustling streets of downtown Chicago is the Pedway — a network of underground tunnels and overhead skybridges connecting more than 40 city blocks in the Loop. Originally developed in the 1950s, the Pedway links major buildings, hotels, shopping centers, CTA stations, and government offices. It is a popular shortcut for commuters and savvy locals, especially during Chicago's icy winters and rainy spring days. While parts of the Pedway are utilitarian, some sections feature art displays, food courts, and unexpected little shops. It's not always perfectly mapped, which adds a bit of a fun, maze-like adventure for visitors looking to explore a side of the city most tourists miss. The Pedway is worth checking out if you want a practical (and slightly quirky) way to navigate downtown without braving the weather.

Chicago CTA "L" Rail System Map

PLANNING YOUR TRIP
TO CHICAGO

Whether you're visiting Chicago for the first time or returning for a deeper dive, a little planning can make a huge difference in how much you enjoy your trip. From picking the best time to go and where to stay, to budgeting and what to pack, this chapter will help you hit the ground running in the Windy City.

Planning ahead of time can significantly enhance your experience in Chicago, ensuring that you make the most of your visit to this vibrant city. By researching and creating an itinerary, you can prioritize must-see attractions, events, and dining options, allowing for a more organized and enjoyable trip. A few of the top attractions in Chicago that are highly recommended for prebooking include the Art Institute of Chicago, which houses an extensive collection of artworks and often experiences long lines. The Chicago Architecture River Cruise is another popular choice, allowing you to explore the city's architectural landmarks from the water, with limited seating available. Skydeck Chicago at Willis Tower is a must-visit for breathtaking views, and prebooking helps you avoid the wait. Additionally, the Museum of Science and Industry offers a rich array of interactive exhibits,

making advance tickets a great way to ensure entry on busy days.

These attractions often have peak times, especially during weekends and holidays, so prebooking secures your spot and enhances your overall experience. Additionally, being aware of seasonal events and festivals can enrich your experience, as you can align your visit with unique local celebrations. Finally, planning your transportation in advance, whether using public transit, rideshares, or even renting bikes, can save time and reduce stress, allowing you to focus on enjoying all that Chicago has to offer.

Chicago has four distinct seasons, and each one offers a different kind of magic. Summers are vibrant and packed with festivals, but they're also the busiest. Spring and fall bring fewer crowds, gorgeous lakefront scenery, and mild weather. Winter? It's cold, but there's a certain charm to the snow-dusted skyline and festive lights. If you're flexible, shoulder seasons (late April to early June and mid-September to October) are ideal.

Spring in Chicago, spanning from March to May, is a delightful season that ushers in mild weather and vibrant blooms throughout the city. This time of year is marked by events like the Chicago Flower & Garden Show, which showcases stunning floral displays, innovative gardening techniques, and expert advice for gardening enthusiasts. Additionally, the city hosts various outdoor festivals that celebrate art, music, and culture, inviting residents and visitors to enjoy street fairs and lively performances. Parks such as Grant Park and Lincoln Park come alive with colorful flowers and lush greenery, providing the perfect backdrop for leisurely strolls, picnics, or outdoor activities. With the return of warmer temperatures, spring is an ideal time to explore Chicago's rich natural beauty while participating in the many engaging events and activities the city has to offer.

Spring in Chicago

Summer in Chicago, spanning from June to August, is characterized by warm weather and a vibrant atmosphere that invites both locals and visitors to partake in a variety of outdoor activities. This season is packed with major festivals, including the iconic Lollapalooza, which attracts music lovers from around the globe, and the Chicago Air and Water Show, showcasing thrilling aerial performances and impressive watercraft displays. Additionally, the Chicago Blues Festival celebrates the city's rich musical heritage, featuring performances by renowned artists. Throughout the summer, numerous neighborhood street festivals, art fairs, and cultural celebrations highlight the diverse communities and traditions that make up the city. Visitors can enjoy lakeside activities, such as sunbathing and water sports, along with the lively scene at rooftop bars that offer stunning views of the skyline. While summer is a fantastic time to explore Chicago, it's important to be prepared for the humidity that can accompany the warm temperatures.

Fall in Chicago, from September to November, is a beautiful season marked by cool, crisp weather and breathtaking fall foliage that transforms the city into a vibrant tapestry of colors. This time of year features an array of exciting events, including Chicago Gourmet, which celebrates the city's culinary scene through tastings, cooking demonstrations, and chef showcases. Families can enjoy festive activities at Lincoln Park Zoo's ZooBoo, where the zoo is transformed into a Halloween wonderland with games and themed decorations. The Renegade Craft Fair presents a marketplace for artisans and crafters, offering unique handmade goods and a chance to support local creators. Additionally, the Chicago International Film Festival attracts film enthusiasts, showcasing a diverse selection of films from around the world. With the pleasant weather, fall is an ideal time to visit museums and indulge in the city's culinary delights, making it a perfect season for exploration and enjoyment.

Fall in Chicago

Winter in Chicago, from December to February, brings cold temperatures and the occasional snow-fall, but it also showcases a unique charm with festive holiday decorations all around the city. Notable events like the Lincoln Park ZooLights transform the zoo into a dazzling display of lights and holiday cheer, making it a popular destination for families and couples alike. Ice skating at Millennium Park is another beloved winter activity, where visitors can glide across the rink surrounded by the stunning backdrop of the city skyline. For those visiting between Thanksgiving and Christmas, the Chicago Christkindlmarket is a must-see. Established in 1996, this cherished annual holiday market held in Daley Plaza captures the essence of traditional German Christmas markets. The market is adorned with twinkling lights and festive decorations, offering a delightful atmosphere filled with the aromas of seasonal foods and drinks. Visitors can savor authentic German treats like bratwurst, pretzels, and mulled wine while browsing through vendor stalls showcasing handcrafted gifts and holiday decorations. With live entertainment featuring holiday music and dance performances, the Christkindlmarket creates an enchanting experience that truly embodies the holiday spirit in Chicago.

What to Pack

Chicagoans joke that you can experience all four seasons in one day - and they're not wrong. No matter the season, layering is your friend.

- Year-round: Comfortable walking shoes, a refillable water bottle, and a portable umbrella.
- Spring/Fall: Light jacket, layers, scarf, or sweater.
- Summer: Sunscreen, sunglasses, breathable clothes.
- Winter: Warm coat, gloves, boots, hat—seriously.

Don't forget your Ventra card if you plan to use the CTA (you can also buy it at the airport or online).

What to Budget

Chicago can be surprisingly affordable - or indulgently expensive - depending on your choices.

- Hotels: $150–300+/night (downtown); less in outer neighborhoods.
- Meals: $10–20 for casual eats; $40–60+ for nice dinners.
- Attractions: Many are free (Lincoln Park Zoo, Millennium Park, public art). Museums range from $15 to $40.
- Transit: A CTA day pass is $5–15 and often cheaper than rideshares.

Want to save? Look for city passes and museum-free days, and walk or ride the L whenever possible.

Free and Budget-Friendly Ideas

- Take a walk along the Lakefront Trail or the 606.
- Visit the Lincoln Park Conservatory or Cultural Center.
- Catch a free concert in Millennium Park during the summer.

- Hop on the water taxi for a cheap, scenic ride.
- Explore neighborhoods like Pilsen or Andersonville - no ticket required.

Safety and City Etiquette

Chicago is a welcoming city, and most tourist areas are safe, especially during the day. Use the same street smarts you would in any large urban area.

- Stick to well-lit areas and main streets at night.
- Keep your valuables secure on public transit.
- If you're lost, most locals are happy to help - just ask.

How Long Should You Stay?

Chicago is a big city that's easy to explore in manageable pieces. Here's a rough guide:

- 1-2 days: Stick to the essentials - Millennium Park, the Loop, a museum, and a river cruise.
- 3-4 days: Add a few neighborhoods, try the food scene, and catch a show or a game.

- 5+ days: Dive into the culture. Try taking a walking tour, hop between neighborhoods, visit hidden gems, or even plan a day trip.

Where to Stay

Chicago is a city of neighborhoods, and where you stay can shape your whole experience. Here's a quick breakdown:

- The Loop: Central, walkable, best for first-timers.
- River North & Gold Coast: Chic, near great dining and shopping.
- Streeterville: Steps from Navy Pier and the lake.
- West Loop: Food lover's dream, hip and energetic.
- Lincoln Park or Lakeview: Great for families, parks, and a neighborhood feel.
- Wicker Park & Logan Square: Artsy, indie, and less touristy.

If you're on a budget, look for accommodations near CTA lines. Avoid staying too far from transit unless you plan to rent a car.

EXPLORING CHICAGO WITH KIDS

Chicago is one of the best big cities in the country to explore with kids. It's packed with hands-on museums, scenic parks, family-friendly restaurants, and just enough quirkiness to keep kids wide-eyed and engaged. Whether you're traveling with toddlers, tweens, or teens, this chapter highlights fun, low-stress ways to experience the city together.

Top Family-Friendly Attractions

Lincoln Park Zoo

Free and centrally located, this zoo is a favorite for locals and visitors alike. There's a great farm-in-the-zoo area, daily animal feedings, and a nearby conservatory with tropical plants and koi fish. Bonus: It's near the lake and has plenty of green space for running around. During the winter months, don't miss ZooLights, one of my favorite Chicago holiday traditions. The zoo transforms into a sparkling wonderland with festive light displays, music, and seasonal treats. It's perfect for kids (and grown-ups) of all ages.

Museum of Science and Industry (MSI)

This museum is an excellent choice for curious kids and grown-ups alike. Kids enjoy the hands-on exhibits (like the mirror maze and tornado chamber), interactive model trains, the coal mine ride, and the U-505 submarine (one of my favorites). MSI dives into real science and engineering for adults, not just surface-level facts. The historical and technological depth of exhibits such as the WW II U-boat, the genetics lab, and the environmental sustainability models fascinate curious adults. Anyone can easily spend hours exploring the exhibits. MSI manages to be both accessible and thought-provoking, making it one of Chicago's most universally loved attractions.

The Field Museum

The Field Museum is kid-friendly because it combines awe-inspiring exhibits with interactive, hands-on experiences that engage children of all ages, while still impressing adults. Some of the top reasons this museum is a favorite for families include SUE the T. rex, gigantic eye-level exhibits, Crown Family Play-Lab (seasonal), Ancient Egypt hall complete with mummies, Pawnee Earth Lodge, and more. There are plenty of restrooms and wide, stroller-friendly pathways. The Field Museum is fascinating for both adults and kids.

Shedd Aquarium

Stingrays, belugas, and penguins - oh my! The Shedd Aquarium isn't just about fish tanks. It is a full-on underwater adventure for kids. It includes interactive touch pools, aquatic shows, colorful exhibits, and plenty of family amenities. The Shedd's interactive exhibits and aquatic shows make it a must-visit. It's also stroller-friendly and easy to combine with a trip to the nearby Field Museum or Adler Planetarium. The Shedd is both magical and manageable, combining discovery with delight. It's often the highlight of the trip for younger visitors.

Maggie Daley Park

Tucked between Millennium Park and the lakefront, this enormous playground is a work of art. Maggie Daley Park is a full-blown urban playground that feels like something out of a storybook. Think towering slides, rope bridges, climbing walls, and even a mini climbing park. During the winter, the skating ribbon is a hit. This park is one of Chicago's top outdoor spaces for kids of all ages to run, climb, explore, and burn off some energy.

Navy Pier

Navy Pier is often considered Chicago's lakefront playground. It is packed with things to see, do, eat, and ride all in one spot. Navy Pier is like a mini amusement park on the lakefront, home to the Centennial Wheel, the Chicago Children's Museum, and many snack stops. Kids love the boat rides and hands-on art activities. Whether you're looking for a whole afternoon of activities or just a fun place to let the kids stretch their legs, Navy Pier delivers.

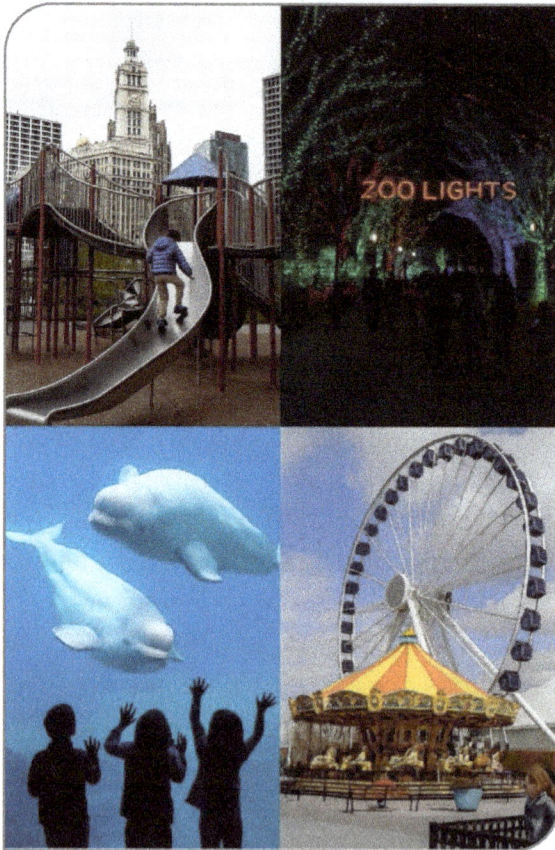

Family-Friendly Chicago Attractions

CONCLUSION

Understanding Chicago's cultural norms can enhance your experience in the city. Chicagoans are often characterized by their resilience, practicality, and strong sense of community. They value honesty and tend to be straightforward in their communication. A great sense of humor is also prevalent among locals. Tipping practices are important here, with a customary tip of 15-20% for service workers in restaurants, bars, and taxis, and more for exceptional service. Sports loyalty runs deep, with passionate fans supporting teams like the Cubs and Sox (MLB), Bears (NFL), Blackhawks (NHL), Chicago Fire (MLS), Red Stars (NWSL), Chicago Sky (WNBA) and Bulls (NBA), making sports discussions a great way to connect with locals. When interacting with Chicagoans, it's important to respect personal space; a little distance in conversation is appreciated, especially in crowded places, but a smile or nod can help establish rapport. Lastly, Chicago is a rich tapestry of cultures, celebrated through various festivals, foods, and community events, so being open to diverse experiences is highly valued.

While you are visiting, you should know Malort (made in Chicago since the 1930s) is Chicago's unofficial mascot, a drink so infamous that trying it is

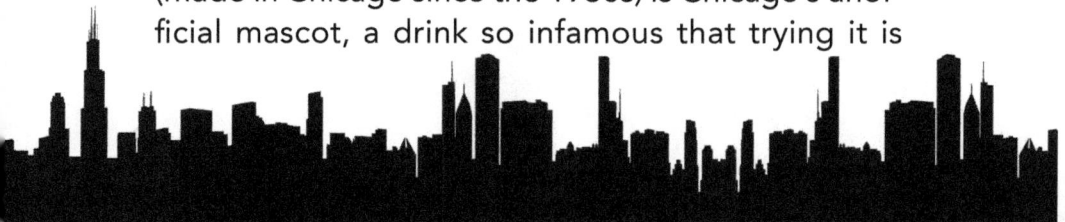

basically a rite of passage for every tourist. Sure, it tastes like burnt rubber mixed with regret, but that's what makes it an essential part of the Chicago experience. Why else would you visit the city and not try the spirit that locals love to *not* recommend? It's a bonding moment in a shot glass—one where you'll instantly know who's truly from Chicago (they'll be smiling through the pain). So, if you want the full Windy City experience, grab a glass of Malort. It's a drink that'll make your taste buds question your life choices while the locals quietly nod, proud you survived it.

Malört

Before I sign off, I want to address a few questions visitors often ask me. First, where can I get the best pizza? Here are a few suggestions:

- Lou Malnati's: Known for its buttery crust and fresh ingredients, Lou Malnati's is a classic choice for deep-dish lovers. Their signature "Malnati Chicago Classic" features a hearty sausage layer and a rich tomato sauce.

- Giordano's: Famous for its stuffed deep-dish pizza, Giordano's offers a unique and delicious take on the traditional style. The stuffed crust is filled with cheese and toppings, creating a delightful balance of flavors.
- Pequod's Pizza: Renowned for its caramelized crust and savory toppings, Pequod's is a favorite among locals. The deep-dish pizza here is baked in a cast-iron pan, giving it a distinctive texture and taste.
- Art of Pizza: A beloved neighborhood spot, Art of Pizza serves both stuffed and pan-style deep-dish pizzas. With generous portions and a variety of toppings, it's a great place for a casual meal.

The second question, why is it called the Windy City? You might think it's all about the fierce gusts blowing off Lake Michigan or the chilly drafts that sneak into your coat, but the truth is a bit more amusing. Chicago earned this nickname not just from the weather, but because of the hot air generated by its politicians back in the day. So, when you're in Chicago, don't be surprised if the wind seems to carry a few tall tales alongside it.

As a lifelong resident of Chicago, I can confidently say that the city offers an incredible blend of culture, history, and vibrant neighborhoods that make it a unique destination for any traveler. Whether you're indulging in our world-class cuisine, enjoying a day at the lakefront, or immersing yourself in the arts, there's something for everyone to enjoy. Remember to explore both the iconic landmarks and the hidden gems that give Chicago its character. Embrace the friendly yet straightforward nature of the locals, and don't hesitate to strike up a conversation. Our city is a melting pot of experiences waiting to be discovered, and I hope this travel guide helps you navigate your journey through the Windy City. Welcome to Chicago!

MAKE A DIFFERENCE WITH YOUR REVIEW

Pass the Spark, Share the City

*"A candle loses nothing by light-
ing another candle."
– James Keller*

If this guide helped you uncover hidden gems, feel more confident exploring new neighborhoods, or fall more in love with the Windy City, would you consider passing that spark to someone else?

To leave a review, just scan the QR code below or visit the review page online. It only takes a moment, but it could help someone else create unforgettable memories.

Thank you for being part of this journey.

RESOURCES

For more information about Chicago's parks, attractions, museums, and travel planning, here are some helpful resources:

- **Choose Chicago** – Chicago's official tourism site.
- Website: *choosechicago.com*
- **Chicago Park District** – Information about parks, beaches, trails, and public gardens.
- Website: *chicagoparkdistrict.com*
- **Chicago Transit Authority (CTA)** – Bus and train maps, fares, and trip planning.
- Website: *transitchicago.com*
- **Field Museum** – Natural history exhibits and special programs.
- Website: *fieldmuseum.org*
- **Shedd Aquarium** – Marine life exhibits and aquatic shows.
- Website: *sheddaquarium.org*
- **Adler Planetarium** – Astronomy exhibits, sky shows, and education programs.
- Website: *adlerplanetarium.org*
- **Art Institute of Chicago** – World-renowned art collections and exhibitions.
- Website: *artic.edu*

- Garfield Park Conservatory – Indoor gardens, tropical exhibits, and seasonal flower shows.
- Website: *garfieldconservatory.org*
- Navy Pier – Dining, entertainment, and waterfront attractions.
- Website: *navypier.org*
- Chicago Riverwalk – Dining, sightseeing, and recreation along the Chicago River.
- Website: *chicagoriverwalk.us*
- Chicago Architecture Center – Tours, exhibits, and resources about Chicago's architectural history.
- Website: *architecture.org*

www.ingramcontent.com/pod-product-compliance
Lightning Source LLC
Chambersburg PA
CBHW062005040426
42447CB00010B/1919